German Armored Trains in World War II Vol.II

 Eisb.Panzerzug   2

 Eisb.Panzerzug   6

 Eisb.Panzerzug   63

 Eisb.Panzerzug   66

 Eisb.Panzerzug   67

 Eisb.Panzerzug   24

Wolfgang Sawodny

Schiffer Military History
Atglen, PA

PHOTO CREDITS:

Federal Archives, Koblenz (BA)
J.Chr. Gembe, Vaterstetten (GE)
Albert Hellrung, Schwelm (HE)
Werner Köhler, Paderborn (KO)
Günter Krause, Werl (KR)
John Loop, Bothell, WA, USA (LO)
Janusz Magnuski, Warsaw, Poland (MG)
Paul Malmassari, St. Maur, France (ML)
Military Archives, Freiburg (MA)
Author's collection (SA) — these were gathered from private albums of former armored train soldiers. The quality of these amateur photos varies considerably and is often deficient in sharpness or contrast.

Drawings: Ulrich Schwarze, Karlsruhe

Translated from the German by Dr. Edward Force, Central Connecticut State University.

Copyright © 1990 by Schiffer Publishing.
Library of Congress Catalog Number: 90-62992.

All rights reserved. No part of this work may be reproduced or used in any forms or by any means—graphic, electronic or mechanical, including photocopying or information storage and retrieval systems—without written permission from the copyright holder.

Printed in China
ISBN: 0-88740-288-7

This book originally published under the title, *Panzerzüge im Einsatz auf deutscher Seite 1939-1945*, by Podzun-Pallas Verlag, GmbH 6360 Friedberg (Dorheim), © 1989. ISBN: 3-7909-0384-1.

Published by Schiffer Publishing Ltd.
4880 Lower Valley Road
Atglen, PA 19310
Phone: (610) 593-1777; Fax: (610) 593-2002
E-mail: Info@schifferbooks.com
Please visit our web site catalog at
www.schifferbooks.com

In Europe, Schiffer books are distributed by
Bushwood Books
6 Marksbury Avenue Kew Gardens
Surrey TW9 4JF England
Phone: 44 (0) 20-8392-8585; Fax: 44 (0) 20-*8392-9876*
E-mail: info@bushwoodbooks.co.uk
Free postage in the UK. Europe: air mail at cost.

This book may be purchased from the publisher.
Include $3.95 for shipping. Please try your bookstore first.
We are always looking for people to write books on new and related subjects.
If you have an idea for a book please contact us at the above address.
You may write for a free catalog.

FOREWORD

The volume "German Armored Trains in World War II", which appeared in 1989 and has been until now the only publication on this special weapon, has gone over so well that it was not only sold out within a short time but attracted attention all over the world. As a result, many former armored train soldiers have contacted me, and with their help and intensive research of my own it has become possible to tell much of the construction and action history of the German armored trains, despite the lack of sufficient official documentation. So I am happy that the publishers have given me the opportunity to present this knowledge, now much more inclusive, in the form of a short outline in a new volume. Since the basis of their development was already presented correctly in the first volume, this general textual structure could be taken over with the newly acquired information worked in, which — aside from the first chapter — required considerable reworking. In the photo section — corresponding to the publishers' principles — new material is offered almost without exception, in which the emphasis is placed rather on service history instead of technical development as in the first volume. Only where corrections were required and could not be made using other photos, were pictures repeated. — The author hopes to be able to offer a brief but informative and significant history of the armored trains. He is working further on a more thorough presentation of this material. For that reason he is still grateful for any additional and corrective information.

ACKNOWLEDGEMENTS

Hearty thanks to all the ladies and gentlemen of the Federal Archives in Koblenz, Freiburg (Military Archives) and Aachen (Central Information Office), the Military History Research Office in Freiburg, the German Service Center (ASt) in Berlin and the Search Service of the German Red Cross in Munich for their cooperation and their active and energetic help in evaluating the contents of their files, to Messrs. Fritz Hahn (Oberkochen), John Loop (Bothwell, WA, USA), Janusz Magnuski (Warsaw), Paul Malmassari (St. Maul) and Jürg Meister (Bonny Hills, Australia) for their generous exchange of ideas and generously provided material, to many railroad experts (above all Mr. Hansjürgen Wenzel (Koblenz), for valuable information and photos, and particularly to Mr. Günther Krause (Werl) and Ulrich Schwarze (Karlsruhe) for their unselfish cooperation over the years. But my special thanks go out to the many former members of armored train units, whom I cannot name for lack of space, who tried to answer my many questions with patience and to the best of their knowledge and ability after such a long time, and who willingly made their still-available photographic and documentary material available to me. Without their cooperation and great help, my work would have had to remain an unsatisfactory fragment.

INTRODUCTION

After the first railroad train puffed from Stockton to Darlington (England) on September 27, 1825, a military significance of this new means of transportation could, of course, be anticipated, but turning theory to practice was only possible after a more or less connected network of tracks had developed in a number of countries. In the process, the advantages it offered for troop and supply transport had been recognized quite early. The possibilities of using railroad rolling stock directly as weapons took longer to develop. To be sure, the Austrians, as early as the revolutionary wars of 1848-49, equipped flatcars with sidewalls of overlapping railroad rails to afford armor protection for the riflemen behind them, and used these cars not only in the siege of Vienna but also in Hungary and northern Italy. In the American Civil War (1861-65) both North and South mounted guns on railroad cars, and the French had already built armored infantry cars, and armed them with Mitrailleuses (the forerunner of the machine gun), by the end of the Sixties. though they were not used in the Franco-Prussian War (1870-71) — though armored railroad batteries, considerably improved in comparison to the American Civil War types, were built and used in besieged Paris — , but the honor of having built the first actual armored train in the modern sense — marked by the union of infantry and artillery — belongs to the British. It was built during the Egyptian campaign of 1882. In subsequent times, similar trains often were used by them in their colonial wars, most frequently (by the end of the war no fewer than 19 such trains existed) and spectacularly in the Boer War (1899-1902). From then on, almost all other nations also built armored trains, and by the outbreak of World War II there was scarcely a warlike dispute in which they did not play a role in one form or another.

The German General Staff also took a lesson from the Boer War and considered the use of armored trains, and soon enough — during the Herero revolt in the colony of Southwest Africa in 1904 — they had a chance to gather practical experience with an improvised unit. This led to the deposition of materials in individual locomotive factories, to be used in case of mobilization for the armoring of a Type 913-18 (Prussian T 93) locomotive and twelve open freight cars per train with steel walls. At the beginning of World War I, nine such armored trains were prepared, at first manned only by infantrymen, and one of them took part in the first act of war, the occupation of Luxembourg. The Germans were probably the only people other than the Russians who already had such units when the war began. Soon the Austrians, Belgians and British (to guard the coasts of the homeland) followed suit. By 1915 the German Reich put six more into service, the Austro-Hungarian Empire a total of eleven armored trains, now carrying artillery weapons (the older trains were rearmed accordingly). As the fronts settled into trench warfare, the possible uses of the armored trains were limited to protective assignments in the homeland. Therefore both Germany and Austria reduced the number of their armored trains by half (seven and five respectively) in 1916-17.

The actual theater of war for armored trains was the territory of the former Russian Empire after the revolution of 1917. In the hostilities that followed, all sides, the Reds, the Whites, the Czechs in Siberia, the allied intervention troops, the Finns, the Poles and the Germans (before the collapse in the Ukraine, and later the Free Corps fighting in the Baltic area), used them, often in massed form, gathered into whole "armored train divisions."

At this time the form of the armored train that was to remain into World War II took shape. It was dominated by the combination of infantry and artillery. The former was armed with light weapons (including machine guns and grenade launchers) and usually included a shock troop that could operate outside the train. Some of the machine guns were built in, and if possible positioned so they could cover the whole train in their fields of both traverse and elevation (it must be kept in mind that the trains could be divided into sections or positioned on causeways), so as to be able to fight off an enemy approach. As for the artillery, guns of lighter calibers (mostly 7.5 to 10.5 cm) were preferred, handily mounted in rotating turrets with a traverse arc of at least 270 degrees. All the cars were armor-plated, as was the locomotive, generally with plating limited to S.m.K. or anti-shrapnel types for the sake of weight. The cars were generally grouped symmetrically, with the locomotive (often with a second tender to extend the range) in the center, with the infantry cars and the command car inside, the latter with effective telephone and radio facilities for communication inside and outside the train, then the artillery cars, so the guns could be brought to bear to the front or rear. At each end of the train was a so-called "Controller" or pusher car, which was supposed to push away mines lying on the tracks or deflect "burners" (freight cars loaded, for example, with explosives) in time to avoid harming the train. They also carried loads of tracklaying equipment with which the engineer troop on the train could repair track damage that hampered the movement of the train. An armored trolley or scout car with railroad wheels for reconnaissance purposes also was usually a part of the armored train, and a supply train was stationed at the depot that served as the train's base of operations.

Thus the armored train was a self-contained combat unit that could operate independently. There were considerable variations in terms of size and strength: the Czechs preferred very small units with just one gun car in front of the locomotive and one infantry car behind it; the Russians and Poles had very strong trains with at least four guns. Depending on these factors, the number of personnel could vary greatly — from 40 to 200 men, but usually about company strength.

As for the potential uses of armored trains, a wide range was seen originally:
Independent offensive tasks:
a. Reconnaissance along the tracks, particularly of railway features (depots, bridges, tunnels, etc.)
b. Taking possession of railway features
c. Breakthroughs into enemy territory
d. Offensive intervention in battles
e. Artillery fire on targets from advance positions
f. Pursuit (and possible capture) of retreating enemy forces

Independent defensive tasks:

a. Blocking enemy advances
b. (Surprise) counterattacks against advancing enemy forces
c. Fighting off enemy tanks
d. Covering retreats as a rear-guard
e. Gathering retreating troop units
f. Defending against enemy raids on transport lines to the rear
g. Coastal defense

Support tasks:
a. Supporting infantry in attack and defense by the effect of weapons, especially artillery
b. Securing flanks of units operating parallel to rail lines
c. Leading attacks in action against terrain obstacles
d. Artillery fighting from covered positions

Czech and Hungarian armored trains — Built 1914-19

Russian armored train — Built 1917-19

Polish armored train — Built 1921

German track protection train — Built 1921 ff.

e. Radio headquarters for operations by mixed battle groups

Securing tasks:
a. Securing and repairing railway features
b. Securing connections to the rear
c. Securing troop concentrations
d. Securing supply depots
e. Securing troop and supply trains during transport
f. Patrol runs for railway surveillance

During the Thirties, serious doubts were raised as to the further utility of armored trains, being bound to the railway network, slow-moving, offering relatively large targets and being expensive to create and maintain. The much smaller and more maneuverable armored wheeled and tracked vehicles seemed to be far superior for combat purposes. There was also the danger of air attacks, in which not only direct hits but also those on the tracks in front and in back of the train could paralyze it. Thus the Poles developed the concept of numerous armored railcars that could operate as needed, whether independently, in groups or in single positions to cover a large extent of track, or could be coupled together to form armored trains with concentrated firepower. This concept, though, did not develop beyond the testing stage before the war began.

Above: Czech armored train (built 1919): the material of the three armored trains of this type was utilized as of 1940 in German armored trains 23 to 25.

Below: Polish armored train "Danuta"; the same types of cars and locomotives were later used in German armored trains No. 10 and 21.(MG, MA)

FROM 1938 TO THE SUMMER OF 1941

In the spring of 1921 the Reichswehr, at the order of the Entente powers, had to disband its 31 existing armored trains. But only a few weeks later the German Reichsbahn was able to obtain from the Allies an agreement to the establishment of so-called "railway protection trains", which were supposed to assure smooth-running railway traffic in case of internal unrest. They consisted of six covered freight cars whose wooden walls were backed by steel plates. Since they had unarmored locomotives at first (only at the end of the Twenties did they receive armored locomotives of the 57 and 93 types — ex-Prussian "G 10" and "T 14" types), they could appear to the casual observer (if he overlooked loopholes and observation positions) as harmless freight trains. Most of the time they stood under cover in sheds, scarcely appearing until the spring of 1933 when, as a result of the burning of the Reichstag and the subsequent wave of arrests, they were brought out to inhibit unrest, attracting attention — favorable from the National Socialist government, disapproving outside the country. Every Reichsbahn administrative district was supposed to maintain such a railway protection train, though there were a number that had none, and others that had several — especially on the eastern border of the Reich. In all, 22 such trains existed in 1937.

In the Thirties, the German military command likewise regarded the armored train as being superseded by the development of air and tank forces. Thus it refused to build new trains and limited itself to taking over seven railway protection trains from the Reichsbahn and rearming them. On July 23, 1938 the OKH sent instructions to the Wehrmacht

districts in which the railway protection trains to be taken over were stationed, but only four of these trains were equipped with additional guns (two 7.5-cm cannons) for combat duty; the other three trains had to make do with their track-protecting equipment of heavy machine guns (08) and were intended only for securing duties. Battle Trains No. 3 and 4 took part in the occupation of the Sudetenland (October 1938) and of the rest of Czechoslovakia (March 1939), but without using their weapons actively. In the latter operation, five Czech armored trains fell into German hands unharmed and without putting up a fight.

In the Polish campaign the attempt to capture the Vistula bridges at Dirschau unharmed, in which Armored Train No. 7 took part, failed; Armored Train No. 3, fighting at the depot in Ponitz, could barely defend itself until the returning troops arrived, and was considerably damaged; Armored Train No. 4 could not even cross the

Pictures at right:
Armored Train No. 6
(formerly Insterburg
Railway Protection
Train, see also Vol. I,
pages 5 and 23,
above).(BA)

border at Wildfurt, Upper Silesia, because the tracks had been destroyed, and only Armored Train No. 6 took part in the successful capture of Grajevo. Subsequent securing duties in the occupied territory, in which the other three armored trains also took part, took place without incident.

In March of 1940 Armored Trains No. 23 to 25 were made up out of captured Czech equipment. In the process, the number of guns was reduced by removal to two (modified 7.5-cm Skoda M 15 L/28 mountain cannons. Trains No. 23 and 24 took part in the occupation of Denmark in April of 1940 and remained there; No. 25 passed through Luxembourg in the western campaign and performed securing service in the Belgian-French border area. — The other German armored trains were placed on Maas and Ijssel bridges in Holland on May 10, 1940, but only Armored Train No. 1 was able to cross the Maas at Gennep and then break through the Peel position, while on its return trip it ran into a barrier that had been closed and was derailed. Armored Train No. 5 remained on the bridge north of Roermond, out of action from being hit in its brake line, and was badly damaged by Netherlands fire.

It was removed later and the equipment that was still usable was used to reconstitute Armored Train No. 1. The latter now received two gun cars, each with a 4.7-cm antitank gun (Böhler/Siderius) and a 2-cm anti-aircraft gun. The other armored trains were also equipped with these anti-aircraft guns, and the gun cars of Armored Train No. 25 were added to Armored Train No. 2.

Armored Trains No. 23 to 25, made up of captured Czech material, were taken out of service in the autumn of 1940, but in June and July of 1940 two armored trains (No. 21 and 22), consisting of captured Polish cars and locomotives, joined the Wehrmacht. These two trains, better equipped in terms of artillery (No. 22 had three 7.5-cm 02/26(p) field cannons, No. 21 had the same plus two 10-cm light F.H. 14/19(p), all in rotating turrets), remained in the General Government at first but were sent to occupied France in the spring of 1941. — At this time, shortly before the Russian campaign began, Armored Trains No. 23 and 24 were reactivated. They were sent to Serbia.

In the winter of 1940-41, though, the building of several new armored trains was considered. In December of 1940, Railroad

Engineer Inspection In 10 presented two designs: "Armored Train 1941", for immediate use, with tanks set on armored railroad cars — later special tank-carrier cars were to be built and the locomotives were also to be armor-plated, and the train would be completed with other cars (kitchen, hospital, and for shock troops — and "Armored Train SP 42", which — pulled by an armored Diesel locomotive — was to include command and infantry cars as well as tank-carrying cars with removable tanks; automatic uncoupling of all cars was also planned.

When planning for the Russian campaign was in its final phases in the spring of 1941, the Chief of Transportation saw a need to have several armored trains built to the wide Russian gauge (1524 mm) and capable of being used near the front. The available normal-gauge (1435 mm) armored trains could, of course, be used on the Russian track network once the gauge of the rails had been changed, as well as in the hinterlands. For this purpose the immediate solution suggested as "Armored Train 1941" was chosen. At first five such trains were to be set up, including, besides the two pusher cars, three armored flatcars with captured French Somua S 35 tanks carried on them. They were to be pulled by Series 57 locomotives converted to broad gauge. The Operations Department suggested that six trains be made up, including open freight cars with low steel walls loopholes for an additional infantry crew. The order to set up these armored trains, No. 26 to 31. was given on May 28, 1941. The trains had two (No. 29-31) or three (No. 26-28) tank-carrier cars with Somua S 35 tanks and one (No. 30, 31) or two (No. 26-29) open infantry cars. The locomotives had armor plate only on their cabs, and for the sixth train a Diesel locomotive of Type WR

Left: The view from a gun car of Armored Train 7 shows the destroyed Vistula bridges at Dirschau on September 1, 1939.(SA)

360 C was converted to broad gauge (these locomotives were used as switch engines in border railroad yards until the trains were made up on the night of June 22, 1941).

At the beginning of the Russian campaign, the armored trains were divided on this front as follows:

Army	Normal Gauge	Broad Guage	Where Stationed
HGr. Nord:			
18. Armee	Nr. 6		Insterburg
16. Armee		Nr.26+30	Eydtkau
HGr. Mitte:			
9. Armee	Nr. 1+3		Ortelsburg
4. Armee	Nr. 2	Nr. 28+29	Warschau, Terespol, Platerow
2. Pz.Gruppe		Nr. 27	Terespol
HGr. Süd:			
6. Armee	Nr. 4+7		Kielce
17. Armee		Nr. 31	Zurawica

Above and right:
Armored Train No. 3 after the battle at Konitz on September 1, 1939. The train went from the station to a blown-up bridge, where the pusher car fell off and the gun car was derailed. The train, thus immobilized, was exposed to heavy Polish fire, traces of which can be seen clearly in the lower picture. The almost undamaged armor plates behind the shattered woden freight-car walls are also easy to see.

Above: Two more pictures of Armored Train No. 3 at Konitz. After being hit by artillery fire, the ammunition in one of the gun turrets blew up.(SA)

Below: The Commander of Armored Train No. 3, Oberleutnant Euen, was killed by this direct hit of an antitank shell on the observation turret on September 1, 1939.(SA)

Right: Armored Train No. 1 on Mat 10, 1940, after breaking through the Peel position in The Netherlands. It was derailed on the return trip by running into a barrier that had been closed.(SA)

Pictures of Armored Train No. 23, assembled from captured Czech rolling stock. Upper left: The train in Denmark in April of 1940, still in Czech camouflage paint. The other pictures show the train later in the Balkan area. Along with the Czech armored cars, two internally armored freight cars (as in the railway protection trains) were added. The locomotive is German, of Series 93 (No. 220). For other pictures see Vol. I, page 9.(1 x ML, 3 x SA)

Armored Train No. 25 also consisted of captured Czech cars (see picture at upper left, which shows it when first set up in the spring of 1940). When taken out of service in the autumn of 1940, its gun cars were added to Armored Train No. 2. When it was reactivated in the winter of 1941, it received additional cars of old World War I Austrian armored trains (cars with rounded roofs as well as those with flak platforms), plus flatcars with removable captured French Somua S 35 tanks (as also used for the auxiliary broad-gauge armored trains built for the Russian campaign). As of 1943 the Somua tanks were replaced by Type 38 (t) Czech tanks, and 7.5-cm cannons were also mounted on the flatcars (lower right; see also Vol. I, page 10, mistakenly identified there as Armored Train No. 24).(1 x KO, 2 x SA, 1 x BA)

Armored Train No. 21 consisted of rolling stock from four Polish armored trains. The pictures show it in three cities. Above: Shortly after it was established, in the summer of 1940; the small gun car is still missing. Center: In France in 1941-42, still with a Polish locomotive; 2-cm anti-aircraft guns on low-side cars in front of a small gun car. Below: In Russia, 1943, a German Series 93 armored locomotive, small gun car: quadruple anti-aircraft guns instead of a gun turret.(SA)

Above: The gun cars of Armored Train No. 21. At left is the streamlined car from the Twenties. In front is the 7.5-cm F.K. 02/26(p), in back the 10-cm light F.H. 14/19(p). At right are the one- and two-turret old-type cars (1918-19). Armored Train No. 22, also consisted of captured Polish equipment, also had such cars (see Vol. I, pp. 7 & 8).(SA)

Lower left: On October 7, 1943 Armored Train No. 21 ran onto a mine between Rechiza and Vassilievici, which caused the front half of the train to be derailed. Lower right: On June 23, 1944 a similar accident occurred to Armored Train No. 21 near Kola (southeast of Minsk).(SA)

Above: From the same Polish rolling stock, which in this case fell into Russian hands in September of 1939 and then was captured by the Germans at Lemberg in June of 1941, Armored Train No. 10 was made; this is Train 10a (see also Vol. I, page 11).(SA)

Left: Front view of the gun turret with the 10-cm light F.H. 14/19(p) of this train.(SA)

Train 10a in action. Left: The Polish-type light field howitzer can be recognized here too. The original observation turrets have been replaced by German tank cupolas, such as were used on Panzer III and IV tanks. On March 16, 1944 this train (meanwhile Armored Train No. 10) was surrounded in Kovel. The picture shows it firing (here the 7.5-cmF.K. 02/26(p)) on the railway station there, where it was badly damaged by bombs on March 21.(1 x SA, 1 x BA)

Below: These two photos from the "Deutsche Wochenschau" of January 1943 show the 7.5-c, F.K. 02/26(p) of Armored Train No. 10b at the times of firing (above) and maximum recoil (below).(BA)

Above and below:
Armored Train No. 10 at first included a second battle train (10b). Its early history was the same as that of Train 10a but went back even farther, for the Poles had captured the gun cars of this train from the Soviets in 1920. Later this train, 10b, became the independent Armored Train No. 11 (see also Vol. I, p. 12, above).(1 x SA, 1 x BA)

SUMMER 1941 TO THE END OF 1942

The fact that the armored trains had played only a subordinate role so far was not attributable only to skepticism as regarded their value — and their action to date was scarcely likely to change that — but also to the unclear circumstances of who was in charge of them.

Their construction and equipping was, according to instructions from the OKH, up to the In 10 (Railroad Engineers) of the General Army Office in cooperation with appropriate sections of the Army Weapons Office (especially WuG 5 and 6). For its crew, each armored train was assigned to a definite military district. The crew, now up to company strength, was drawn from the most varied troop units (infantry, artillery, anti-aircraft, railroad engineers, intelligence, smokelaying and medical units), which handicapped quick teamwork as well as obtaining replacements. The technical crew of an armored train (a Reichsbahn inspector as technical leader, two engine drivers, three firemen, two track observers and one motor and light mechanic, simultaneously wagon-master) were, until the end of the war, provided at request from the German Reichsbahn via the transport service agencies of the Reich Transport Ministry.

Although railroad engineers and the Chief of Transportation claimed the responsibility for the armored trains, they amounted, according to instructions from the OKH as to equipment and personnel, to general army troops in terms of command; they were subordinated to appropriate troop units for service.

Understandably, the railroad engineers had no great interest in a weapon that they had to equip but that was then removed from their influence; and in the OKH a special unit of not even 2000 men in all, and whose value was still disputed, was necessarily of minor importance.

Yet the Railroad Engineer Inspection In 10 had presented two designs for new armored trains in December of 1940. The short time remaining before the Russian campaign, of course, allowed only the realization of the extremely makeshift immediate solution called "Armored Train 1941" in the form of the broad-gauge trains, No. 26 to 31. The Chief of the Army General Staff saw the necessity of setting up a separate unit for the armored trains. Thus in July of 1941 the position of Staff Officer of Railway Armored Trains was created. Ar first it was to be subordinate to the Chief of Transportation and thus the General of the Railway Troops, but then, as ordered on August 9, 1941, it was assigned to the General of the Fast Troops. The position was given to Oberstleutnant (later Oberst) Egon von Olszewski, who held it until the dissolution of the position on March 31, 1945.

With that the armored trains finally left the realm of the railway troops (although the In 10 was still in charge of their railroad technology). The reasons for this sudden change of control are unknown and even seem contradictory in view of the facts that until then the armored trains had proved to be scarcely suitable for offensive use, and that from this time to the end of 1942 they were used almost exclusively for securing transport routes against ever-increasing partisan activity. On the other hand, there is probably reason for suspecting that the armored train weapon, as part of the railway troops, would scarcely have made the progress that it was to experience under the aegis of the Fast Troops (later armored troops). But the first effects of this could be seen only in 1942.

First of all, the Russians — traditionally inclined to use armored trains and equipped with many of them — demonstrated that this weapon definitely had its merits for defensive use. Of course many were put out of action by the German Luftwaffe, artillery and tanks, but on the southern front in particular, where many of them often went into battle together in the manner of "armored train divisions", they gave the German troops a lot of trouble, such as in the unsuccessful attempt to seize the isthmus of Perekop or in the attack and defensive fighting in the Rostov area in the autumn of 1941.

It is not surprising, what with all their action, that a goodly number of Russian trains were captured at the foremost front during the German advance. Their rolling stock was quickly put to practical use by the Germans. The commanders of Armored Trains No. 23 to 31, which were primitive and fully unsuited to the Russian winter, tried to get their hands on such captured cars; some of them settled for providing weather-tight quarters for their infantry troops in closed cars (Trains No. 26, 30 and 31), others (No. 27 to 29) equipped their trains mightily with armored gun cars, and in some cases armored Russian Series O locomotives were used. Armored Train No. 6 too, which had been damaged in May of 1942, was given such captured cars with four 7.62-cm 295/l(r) field cannons. Other captured rolling stock was used by German railroad and securing troops to set up their own (and thus not subordinate to the OKH and the Staff Officer of the Railroad Armored Trains) auxiliary armored trains. These can be traced back to as early as 1940; their equipment and personnel naturally varied very much. Often they were freight cars provisionally "armored" with sandbags, concrete walls and the like, armed only with infantry weapons (machine guns, grenade launchers, antitank guns); for combat use, anti-aircraft guns (2-cm, later also 8.8-cm cannons) mounted on open cars were popular. Later — as already noted — captured Russian armored-train cars were used, but these were usually called in after a time by the OKH as captured materials to be administered centrally; later — though in very rebuilt form — they generally served to upgrade the older regular armored trains. They were replaced by "homemade" armored bodies on freight cars, topped with the turrets of captured but no longer driveable Russian tanks. If these turrets came from T 34 tanks, then the makeshift armored trains were often superior in firepower to the official ones. In order to avoid confusion, they could only be called "track protection trains" according to a directive of the OKH dated July 12, 1943. They were given a wide variety of names: One finds numbers as well as capital letters, personal names ("Blücher", "Rübezahl"), first names ("Max", "Werner") or place names ("Zobten", "Berlin", "Stettin"). Sometimes it happened that such trains were taken into the series of official armored trains: On June 16, 1942 the auxiliary armored train "Stettin" or "A" (with four 4.5-cm KwK guns in Russian BT-7 tank turrets) became Armored Train No. 51, and on June 1, 1944 the Track Protection Train "Blücher" became Armored Train No. 52. In March of 1945, in view of a lack of sufficient new construction, a whole row of Track Protection Trains were legitimized at one stroke ("Berlin", "Max", "Moritz", "Werner", No. 83 and No. 350).

Auxiliary armored trains also existed in areas in which no regular ones saw service, for example, in Norway (the trains

The auxiliary broad-gauge armored trains prepared for the Russian campaign, that consisted only of tank-carrying cars with removable captured French Somua S 35 tanks, infantry cars open at the top, and a Series 57 locomotive with only its cab armored. Above is Armored Train No. 28 (Army Group Center).(1 x SA, 1 x BA)

"Norwegen", "Voss", "Grong" and "Narvik"), and toward the end of the war the increasing numbers of such trains were seen as a means of making heavy weapons mobile despite the lack of gasoline.

Along with the aforementioned Armored Train No. 51 (sent to Army Group North to replace the withdrawn Armored Train No. 6), only two more regular armored trains reached the troops in 1942. In December of 1941 Armored Train No. 25, which had been out of service for more than a year, was reactivated and equipped with rebuilt old Austro-Hungarian cars (captured from the successor states) in place of the gun cars added to Armored Train No. 2, with modified 7.5-cm Skoda M 15 L/28 mountain cannon were placed in open mounts. This armored train was first sent to the back-line area of the central sector of the eastern front, and in October of 1942 it was exchanged for Armored Train No. 21 and sent to France. Early in 1942 two broad-gauge armored trains, captured from the Russians in Lemberg after the Russians had taken them from the Poles in 1939, were put into service. They were given No. 10 and set up as a unit similar to one of the Russian armored train divisions, each train having four guns, and were first used in the Byelgorod-Kharkov area. In 1943 the two trains were separated, one retaining No. 10 and the other becoming Armored Train No. 11.

The armored trains on the eastern front followed the battle troops in two echelons during the advance: near the front were the broad-gauge No. 26 to 31, farther back (after the tracks were converted to normal gauge) were Armored Trains No. 1 to 4, 6 and 7. The distribution of the trains at the beginning of December 1941 corresponded to that in effect when the campaign began: in Army Group North, No. 30 was behind the Leningrad front, No. 6 in the Dno-Novgorod area and No. 26 between Novosokolniki and Dno; in Army Group Center, No. 1 and 2 were in the Polozk-Orcha-Vitebsk-Smolensk area, No. 27, 28 and 29 in the Bryansk-Orel-Jursk area; in Army Group South. No. 4 was between Dnyepropetrovsk and Saporoshye, No. 31 between Krementshug and Poltava.

The Russian December offensive of 1941 also involved the armored trains. On January 2, 1942 No. 27 lost all its cars south of Suchinitski, but was immediately supplied with captured Russian cars in Roslavl; No. 29 had to be destroyed west of Kaluga on January 13, 1942. Armored Trains No. 1 and 2 had all they could do to keep the line from Smolensk to Vyasma, important for supplying the 4th Armored and 9th Armies, while a railway protection train hastily equipped with anti-aircraft guns operated between Vyasma and Rshev (later Armored Train No. 1 was transferred there). Early in 1942, supplying the 83rd Infantry Division, alone in a broad valley near Velikiye Luki, became a problem. Armored Trains No. 3 and the newly established No. 27 secured the route from Nevel, while two railroad protection trains covered that from Novosokolniki. In May of 1942 both armored trains (No. 3 and 27) were badly damaged by mines and withdrawn for repairs. To replace them, the 83rd Infantry Division prepared a railroad protection train that bore the division's number. At the same time Armored Train No. 6 must have been damaged in the Dno area, for it was withdrawn for reequipping about that time.

A view from the tender of broad-gauge Armored Train No. 30 on a line leading through the endless forests of northern Russia.(BA)

In the spring of 1942 the conversion of the Russian railway lines to standard gauge reached the areas near the front. Thus the broad-gauge armored trains had no mobility any more. Between April and August of 1942 they were therefore converted to standard gauge. This was also done to the armored trains with Army Group South (No. 10, 28 — transferred there from Orel in March of 1942 — and 31), although the offensive was in progress there, with the anticipated considerable gain of additional broad-gauge lines. In fact, none of the armored trains with Army Group South (later A and B) took part in it; they all remained in the Kharkov area.

In mid-November of 1942 — as the Russian Stalingrad offensive was beginning — the armored trains were divided as follows: No. 26 and 51 with Army Group North, No. 1, 2, 3, 4 and 21 with Army Group Center, No. 7, 10 and 28 with Army Group B, No. 6 and 24 in the Balkans and No. 22 and 25 in France. Army Trains No. 23, 30 and 31 had been transferred home for rebuilding shortly before, and after undergoing the same, No. 27 was sent to Army Group Center shortly afterward.

Meanwhile the steadily increasing activity of Russian partisans in the back-line army areas had made the securing of the railway lines, the protection of troop and supply transport running on them, and the active fighting of these hard-to-catch groups by far the most important tasks of the armored trains, and had resulted in a growing awareness of the need to strengthen this weapon.

Although the armored trains were mentioned only briefly and generally in the OKW's battle instructions for fighting partisans, issued on November 11, 1942, a whole section — based on experience — of

Two more pictures of Armored Train No. 30. The picture above gives an excellent view into an infantry car, whose armored walls offered protection only to men lying down. The lower picture shows the unloading of a Somua tank on an automatically lowering ramp.(BA)

the OKW memo "Fighting Bands" of May 6, 1944 was devoted to them, and much information on this subject can be found in it. Most appropriate to the uniqueness of the armored trains was their effectiveness in large-scale operations against partisans (in moves with independent combat assignments, cooperation with units that could be disembarked, blocking of partisan escape routes across railway lines, artillery support or use as command posts for operational staffs) and carrying out independent small operations (such as pursuit commands). Also mentioned were: intervention in attacks on transport and on railway lines, securing missions involving secrecy and camouflage, escorting important transport, messenger and special trains, supplying combat support points along the railway lines, assisting in successful attacks, securing threatened railway features and work on and in the vicinity of the tracks, transport of infantry units (up to company strength behind the armor protection of the train itself, otherwise in additional cars), and distribution of propaganda material.

In view of this increase in significance, the establishment in the summer of 1941 of a central troop office with the Staff Officer of Railway Armored Trains under the General of the Fast Troops in the OKH was especially advantageous. His activity showed its first visible effects in the spring of 1942. On April 1, 1942 the Railway Armored Train Replace-ment Unit was founded in Warsaw-Rembertow, at which, after In 6 and 10 of the AHA had finished equipping it, organization, training, replacement refreshing and repair of armored trains was centralized. On May 24, 1942 the General of the Fast Troops gave out the "Temporary Guidelines for Structuring and Utilization of Railroad Armored Trains" issued by the Staff Officer of Railway Armored Trains. Most significant, though, was the concept of a uniform armored train formed in cooperation with In 6; with a few modifications, it was produced until the war ended. The older armored trains were modified in 1943-44 to match this standard in terms of armaments and crews.

These auxiliary broad-gauge armored trains with their open infantry cars were naturally very unsuitable for the Russian winters. Thus attempts were made to improve the situation through the use of captured Russian rolling stock. The most successful of them was Armored Train No. 28, which by the autumn of 1941 had added a complete heavy Russian armored train (two gun cars, each with a 10.7-cm field gun and an armored O Series locomotive). Of the original stock, only the tank-carrier cars with the Somua tanks were retained; the infantry cars and the German locomotive were turned over to the supply train.(BA)

Left: With the conversion to standard gauge in the early summer of 1942, this captured Russian rolling stock was called in by the OKH. Armored Train No. 28 now ran again with its old locomotive, still only partly armored, and the old infantry cars, now at least closed in by slanted roofs, were put back into service. Two ex-Russian gun cars of a different type were added.(SA)

Below: In these gun cars, which originally had two turrets, one of the turrets was replaced by an anti-aircraft position (quadruple 2-cm guns). In the remaining gun turret there is not the usual 7.62-cm F.K. 295/1(r) cannon, but a 4.5-cm Pak 37(r) antitank gun. Behind it is one of the old infantry cars which had been roofed over and, as the antenna on the roof indicates, is now serving as a command car.(SA)

Right: Armored Train No. 28 on the shore of the Sea of Azov near Berdyansk in the spring of 1943.(SA)

Right: Armored Train No. 27 had been surrounded at Suchinitski in January of 1942 and lost its cars. After being liberated, it was supplied with twin-turret captured Russian cars at Roslavl and, along with Armored Train No. 3, was sent to the Nevel-Velikiye Luki line to protect the supplying of the 83rd Infantry Division there (not Armored Train No. 28, as has often been stated in the literature!) On May 30, 1942 it was badly damaged by exploding mines there. The explosion of the forward gun car cost four crewmen, including the commander, their lives.(SA)

Below: Only single captured Russian cars were used in some of the other broad-gauge armored trains. Armored Train No. 26 (left) used a former gun car, one of whose turrets had been rebuilt into an anti-aircraft position, and the gun was removed from the other. In Armored Train No. 31 (right) a large four-axle infantry car was already in use in the winter of 1941-42.

As of the end of 1942, all the older armored trains still in service were rebuilt to a uniform pattern based on the K.St.N./K.A.N. of the standard-type BP 42. The gun cars were new superstructures on captured Russian four-axle chassis, carrying two turrets at different heights. In between was space for the crew and ammunition, plus an observation post. Then came the command car (a freight car with inside armor plate and an observation post) and an anti-aircraft car with quadruple 2-cm guns. A tank carrier car (either a flatcar with side aprons, converted from broad gauge, or a basin-shaped BP 42 type) with a 38(t) tank and a pusher car completed each half of the train. Despite the uniform pattern, these trains showed individual characteristics in certain details. Above: Armored Train No. 1 as of August 1943. Center: Armored Train No. 23 as of August 1943. Below: Armored Train No. 26 as of February 1944.(SA)

 Eisb.Panzerzug 11

 Eisb.Panzerzug 23

In the German breakthrough across the isthmus of Perekop to the peninsula of Crimea early in November 1941, two Russian armored trains were captured. One of them was soon put to use by the Germans (above). It saw its first action north of Feodosia on New Year's Eve, 1942. The train's further fate is unknown.(GE)

Above: The rail protection train formed in the early summer of 1942 by the 83rd Infantry Division bore the division's number as its own designation. It included two armored cars with the turrets of Russian BT-7 tanks (4.5-cm KwK) and remained in action until May of 1945.(HE)

Left: The track protection train "Michael", which saw service in Crimea from November 1943 until its destruction in May of 1944, appears to have had complete T-34/76F tanks with cast iron turrets set on flatcars and surrounded by armor plate. In front is an anti-aircraft gun car armored with sheet steel.(MG)

Left and below:
The Series 200 standard-gauge track protection trains used in Greece and Yugoslavia (see also Vol. I, page 22) had armor-plated infantry cars of unknown (Yugoslavian?) origin as well as captured French tanks, generally old Renault FT 17/18 but also a few Hotchkiss, Renault and Somua medium tanks, carried on low-sided cars.(BA)

Below: Some track protection trains were renamed as regular armored trains, as was the "Stettin" or "A" train, which became Armored Train No. 51 in June of 1942. It had two gun cars, each with two BT-7 tank turrets, giving it the typical appearance of a track protection train (left). At right is the track protection train "Blücher" in the spring of 1944. In October of the same year it became Armored Train No. 52, but the extent of its revised or added equipment is not known.(SA)

NEW ARMORED TRAINS AND RAILCARS

In contrast to the In 10 designs of December 1940, the In 6 tried to make its Uniform Armored Train BP 42 (not EP 42, as is often stated in the literature) able to handle any eventuality of armored train use. Thus the numerically strong infantry crew was retained, and at the same time the artillery was increased, on the Polish and Russian model, to four guns, but not mounted as they were, with two per car, but singly in specially constructed ten-sided rotating turrets, so as to avoid too-great losses when a car was hit. The two halves of the train, before and behind the locomotive running in the middle (usually a Series 57 (G10)), were identical, and each consisted (in order from the locomotive out) of a gun car with a 10-cm light field howitzer 14/19(p), which also contained the kitchen and medical section, a command and infantry car, and a gun and flak car with a 7.62-cm F.K. 295/1(r) and quadruple 2-cm anti-aircraft guns (though there were also trains in which all four guns were of the same type, either 7.62 or 10 cm). All the cars were covered with sloping armor plate (15 to 30 mm) that also protected the wheels. The locomotives also had smooth armor at some distance from their bodies, unlike the "skin-tight", complicated type often used before that had many angles that caught shells; the new type not only offered passageways behind the armor, but also gave better protection.

A feature of the In 10's "Armored Train 1941" plan that had been tested in that group's immediate solution, the broad-gauge Armored Trains No. 26 to 31, and had proved itself, was also retained for BP 42: the tanks loaded on flatcars and easily removable via ramps, by which the battle group that could operate outside the train (previously only

infantry, some of them on bicycles) was significantly strengthened and their radius of action markedly extended. Thus two such new pan-shaped tank-carrier cars with tanks on them (usually Praga T-38(t) with a 3.7-cm KwK and two machine guns) were placed at the ends of the Armored Train BP 42.

The scout cars too — formerly a railcar that could run only on rails and a rail motorcycle — were also improved on. Instead of them, every Armored Train BP 42 received two Panhard 38 (f) (P 204) scout cars, each with a 2.5-cm KwK and a machine gun, usable not only on rails but also — after a ten-minute wheel change — on the road. In part, the old

armored trains were also gradually equipped with such removable tanks and Panhard armored scout cars.

In the BP 42 they had certainly created a strongly armed, imposing-looking armored train, as is often the case with all-around solutions, but in practice it showed weaknesses in all types of action. For fighting partisans the train was too unhandy and not mobile enough, yet on the other hand it was too heavily armed. Before it ponderously set itself in motion, local railroad men had generally informed the partisans of its coming and thus given them the opportunity to disappear — or worse yet (and more and more

often as the war progressed) to construct a mine trap, which led to correspondingly high losses of material. In combat it was at best the equal of enemy infantry, but against the tanks that usually opposed it in Russia it had no armor-piercing weapons to use, while it itself, with its thin armor that protected it only from infantry weapons and shrapnel (and which could not be increased because of axle pressure), was helplessly exposed not only to tank guns but also to antitank guns and similar weapons, even offering a huge target that was hard to miss. Most unthinkable was its use as railroad artillery — and it was used thus often enough — but in this kind of action the rest of its crew was useless (the tanks, to be sure, were often used as mobile and yet somewhat protected B positions). — To increase its fighting strength, the BP 42 was developed further into the BP 44 in the spring of 1944. Of course the limitations on axle pressure prevented any noteworthy improvement in armor plate,

but now there were so-called Panzerjäger cars placed before the tank-carrier cars — flatcars with a Panzer IV turret with a 7.5-cm KwK L/48 (or in isolated cases the turret of a T 34 with a 7.62-cm KwK), in order to offer at least a little opposition to Russian tanks. The intended artillery weapon was the 10.5-cm Field Howitzer 18M (in the same type of turret as on the BP 42). To increase the effect further, a reorganization of the crew (without any great change in numbers) was undertaken. The transition from BP 42 to BP 44 began with Armored Train No. 73 in the spring of 1944. but at first it lacked field howitzers of the intended German type, so that at first the 7.62-cm Field Cannon 295/1(r) and the 10-cm Field Howitzer 14/19(p) were still used, and Armored Trains No. 74 and 75 had to be rushed into action in such a hurry in July of 1944 that they were still lacking the Panzerjäger cars as well. So it was Armored Train No. 76 that first conformed fully to the new plan. In January of 1945 there was

another tight spot in delivery of the 10.5-cm light Field Howitzer 18M; Armored Train No. 79 had to go into battle without gun turrets, and heavy 12-cm grenade launchers were provisionally set in the turret holes of the car bodies.

In 1943 the concept that had been discussed in Poland before the war but also had advocates in Germany was taken up again, after having been suggested as the final stage in the "Armored Train 1941" plan of In 10: motor-driven, armed and armored railcars that could operate singly, in groups of several single units, or coupled together to form a train. Heightened flexibility and greater mobility were expected from such units. From these considerations there originated the le.Sp. (light scout car, Sp = Spähwagen) and s.Sp. (heavy scout car) railroad armored trains. The armored train (le.Sp.) consisted of ten rail scout cars, each driven by an air-cooled Steyr motor of 76 HP (top speed 70 kph), with an armament of four light

The uniform Type BP 42 armored train developed in 1942, shown at left on a siding built for test firing at the Rembertow drill facility (near Warsaw, where the armored train replacement unit was located). At right is a similar train in Russia during the winter of 1943-44.(SA)

machine guns, a six-man crew, armor plate 14.5 mm thick and a weight of 8 tons. It was intended especially for the light roadbeds in southern Serbia, Macedonia and Greece and proved itself splendidly there for track securing, but was naturally of use only for this purpose because of its light armament. The four completed units (No. 301 to 304) reached the troops in the spring of 1944. — The armored train (s.Sp.) was to consisted of twelve rail scout cars variously equipped: a command car (company troop, radio and medical personnel), a command car for the infantry platoon (platoon troop, built-in machine gun), two infantry cars (each with a built-in machine gun, plus a total of one heavy and four light machine guns and two 8-cm grenade launchers), one engineer car (with one built-in and two more machine guns plus flamethrowers), a command car for the artillery platoon (one machine gun), four gun cars with Panzer III N turrets and short 7.5-cm KwK L/24, and two anti-aircraft cars with 2-cm quadruple guns. At the ends of the train there were also tank-carrier cars with Praga 38(t) tanks and pushers, plus a rail-riding Panhard 38(f) scout car for reconnaissance. The individual rail scout cars had 20-mm armor and a total weight of some 18 tons (depending on equipment). They were driven by the same 76-HP Steyr motor as the lighter vehicles. Because of this weak powerplant, the heavy scout cars could only attain a speed of 40 kph.

In all, the fighting strength of the armored train (s.Sp.) was about equal to that of the BP 42, but the debarkable infantry group of 25 men was only about half as large, yet the range (though at a speed decreased by 20 kph) was considerably greater. It was a great advantage that every car had its own power, so that a direct hit on the locomotive could

The front half of a heavy scout train (as delivered as of November 1944). Originally it was to consist of twelve cars with individual powerplants, but it actually was made up of only eight cars, of which the two gun cars were equipped with Panzer III N turrets (with 7.5-cm KwK short).(SA)

not, as before, cripple the whole train. Its combat possibilities were also more varied. The infantry cars could be placed farther forward, the gun cars farther back as a supporting railroad battery and thus less exposed to enemy action. Although ten armored trains (s.Sp.) were planned for just the first half of 1944, the first two (No. 201 and 202) only reached the troops in the Balkans in November of 1944. No. 203 and 204 followed in January of 1945. No. 205 and 206 were delivered to the armored train replacement unit in Milowitz shortly before the war ended. No. 207 and 208 were still at the factory in Steyr, partly finished, and the building of No. 209 and 210 had been

cancelled in January of 1945. The major delays in building these trains was caused by technical difficulties as well as lack of materials. From the start, they were delivered in reduced form: two of the four gun or grenade-launcher cars were lacking, and the quadruple anti-aircraft guns were mounted on low-side cars instead of scout cars. In particular, the late production of the heavy scout trains meant that their truly new features never emerged. Because of a lack of fuel, the scout cars' individual motors could scarcely be used; an unarmored steam locomotive had to be used to move the train in the old familiar way.

Along with the armored trains, there were

Light Scout Train No. 303 in June of 1944, loaded on flatcars for delivery to the Balkan area.(SA)

Three cars of Light Scout Train No. 303. The complete train consisted of ten cars of this type, usually used singly or in pairs (for mutual assistance).(SA)

also armored railcars. Of the five track protection railcars available in the early Thirties (VT 807 to 811), only one — that of the RBD in Königsberg — was on hand when the war began. It was taken over by the Wehrmacht as Armored Railcar No. 15 and remained in service until the war ended. It was armed only with machine guns. — For the "Armored Train SP 42" of In 10, a Wehrmacht WR 550 D Diesel locomotive was equipped with armor plate at the Berliner Maschinenbau AG (Schwartzkopff) in Wildau in 1942; on each side a flak platform, supported by four axles and carrying quadruple 2-cm anti-aircraft guns, was built. Since the "Armored Train SP 42" was not

continued, the anti-aircraft guns were replaced by uniform rotating turrets (as on BP 42) with 7.62-cm 295/l(r) cannons, and the vehicle was put into service at the beginning of 1944 as Armored Railcar No. 16. It was captured by Polish units near Neu-Ruppin early in May of 1945 and is in the Warsaw Railroad Museum today, one of the few formerly German rail vehicles to be preserved. Even before — in December of 1943 — a captured Russian train, likewise with two 7.62-cm guns in rotating turrets, was taken over as Armored Railcar No. 17. It was followed by six more vehicles of the same kind (No. 18 to 23, established between November 1943 and January 1944, but only

reaching the troops in the latter half of 1944).

Along with the two aforementioned guns, these railcars had four machine guns, a 21-man crew and 20-mm armor; they weighed 34 tons each, and an eight-cylinder, 180-horse-power motor gave them a top speed of 60 kph; their range was 500 kilometers. In the spring the Italian firm of Ansaldo-Fossati contracted to build nine armored railcars (Littorine blindate) of Type ALn-56, of which it had formerly built five for the Italian Army, for the German Wehrmacht (Railcars No. 30 to 38). They had two Italian M 13/40 tank turrets with 4.7-cm KwK, a 2-cm (Breda) anti-aircraft gun, and six machine guns (two of them anti-aircraft guns). They first saw service in the

Balkans during the latter half of 1944. As of the winter of 1944-45, three more so-called Panzerjäger railcars (No. 51 to 53) were built; they had the same equipment (though a different appearance) as Railcars No. 18 to 23, except for having rotating turrets of Panzer IV/H with 7.5-cm KwK L/48 instead of the earlier turrets with 7.62-cm cannons. At least one was finished at the factory but was still at the Steyr works when the war ended. The armored railcars were assigned to armored trains to strengthen them. Only Railcar No. 15 operated independently for a time in Greece, with several Panhard scout cars subordinated to it — before the first light scout train was ready for service. Armored Gun Railcars No. 16 to 23 supported armored trains on the eastern front, while the Italian-built railcars (No. 30 to 38) were intended to serve in pairs as escorts for the light scout trains. But only No. 30 and 31 reached Scout Train No. 303 on schedule. The others were assigned to other armored trains in the Balkan area; No. 36 remained in Bohemia and Moravia, while No. 37 reached the eastern front in February of 1945.

At left is the former Track Protection Railcar No. 15. From August 1943 to February 1944 it was used in Greece as a separate entity, with six Panhard scout cars.

At right is Armored Railcar No. 16. This was originally planned as a Diesel locomotive for an armored train. With its 550 horsepower and 100-mm side armor plate, it was the most heavily armored railway vehicle of the German Wehrmacht.(SA)

Captured Russian vehicles served as Armored Railcars No. 17 to 23, two of which can be seen in the pictures to the left and right.(SA)

Below: Made in Italy (by Ansaldo) were the four-axle, twin-engine railcars, No. 30 to 38. Their main armament consisted of two M 13/40 tank turrets with 4.7-cm KwK guns.(KR)

Lower right: The Panzerjäger railcars (No. 51 ff.) with Panzer IV turrets (7.5-cm KwK, long) were finished before the war ended, but they never got into service. The Americans found them as seen here at the factory in Steyr when the war ended.(LO)

The first four armored trains of the BP 42 standard type. Above: Armored Train No. 61 in December of 1942, during testing at Rembertow. Right: Armored Train No. 62 in action near Stanislau (March 1944). Below: Armored Train No. 63 stopped on a bridge in the Volkov area in the summer of 1943. Lower right: Armored Train No. 64 in Croatia during the winter of 1943-44.(SA)

Right: The transition to the improved Type BP 44 was supposed to begin with Armored Train No. 73 (June 1944). But the intended 10.5-cm Light Field Howitzer 18M was not yet ready at first, and the earlier captured guns were used further. When Armored Train No. 74 (shown here) had to be pressed into service hastily in July of 1944 after the Russian breakthrough between the Bug and the Vistula, even the Panzerjäger cars were still lacking.(SA)

Below: Armored Train No. 78 in southwestern Hungary in the spring of 1945. It corresponded fully to the pattern for BP 44. As of early 1944, the armored trains were almost always camouflaged — to prevent being spotted from the air as well as by enemy ground forces.(SA)

Above: The Panzerjäger cars (seen here without the usual vertical armor aprons around the turret and hull), with Panzer IV turret and long 7.5-cm KwK, were an important innovation of the BP 44 train type. They were meant at least to improve the active protection against Russian tanks, after the passive — stronger armor — could not be increased on account of the weight.(SA)

The guns of the BP 42 armored train. At left is the 7.62-cm 295/l(r) field cannon, the Russian M 02/30 with the shorter L/30 barrel (Vo 635 m/sec, maximum range 12 km); at right the Skoda 14/19 10-cm light field howitzer, from captured Polish and probably also from Czech material (Vo 395 m/sec, maximum range 9.8 km).(BA)

Left: For the BP 44 armored train, they were intended to be replaced by the 10.5-cm M 18M light field howitzer (Vo 540 m/sec, maximum range 12.3 km). Right: The actual upgrading, though, was in the form of the added Panzerjäger cars with their 7.5-cm KwK L/48 (Vo 790 m/sec).(1 x BA, 1 x SA)

After good experiences with them in the broad-gauge armored trains, the standard BP 42 (as was the later BP 44) was also equipped with two tank-carrier cars with removable Prage 38(T) tanks. The tub-shaped cars plus a folding armored shield protected the running gear. To remove the tank, the pusher car ahead had to be uncoupled; an automatic Scharfenberg coupling was provided. The pictures above and at left show three stages of unloading. At right is the "face" of the 38(t) tank. With its 3.7-cm KwK and thin armor, it was not the equal of an enemy tank as of 1942, but was well suited to use against partisans because of its good cross-country performance.(3 x SA, 1 x BA)

As a reconnaissance vehicle, as of the end of 1942 the armored trains used only the Panhard 38(f) scout cars captured in France in 1940; they had 105-HP rotary engines and 2.5-cm KwK guns. They could be changed from rail to road wheels or back in about 15 minutes. The pictures above and at the left show them in roadgoing form, being altered and running on rails. At right the road wheels, which the scout cars could not carry with them, loaded on the pusher car of the armored train.(3 x SA, 1 x BA)

FROM 1943 TO THE WAR'S END

According to an OKH directive of July 17, 1942, the first six armored trains of the uniform BP 42 type (No. 61 to 66) were set up in pairs in September, October and November 1942. The first (No. 61) was ready for service after just four months and was sent to the 201st Sich.Div. of Army Group Center, No. 62 to Army Group South in the Kharkov area in February of 1943, and No. 63 to Army Group North in the back-line area of the 18th Army in May. —Meanwhile a critical situation had developed in the Balkans. The constantly increasing partisan activity became more and more of a danger to the main supply line of the German troops in Greece, the Agram-Saloniki-Athens line, and the line between Agram and Belgrade became more and more often the target of such attacks. Thus in 1942 not only Armored Trains No. 23 and 24, previously stationed in Serbia, had to be transferred there, but they were strengthened in the autumn of 1942 by Armored Train No. 6. But after Armored Train No. 23 was withdrawn for rebuilding in October of 1942 and Armored Train No. 23 was put out of action in February of 1943, the situation became very precarious. At first temporary measures were taken with — besides two available narrow-gauge Croatian armored trains — the preparation of track protection trains, of which there were five in the Croatian area and four in Greece in July and August of 1943. But in June and July of 1943 the OB Southeast also received two new trains of the BP 42 uniform type, No. 64 and 65. It turned out, of course, that they were too heavy for the southern Serbian, Macedonian and Greek tracks. This was the reason why the planning of the light and heavy scout trains began in August and September, of

which the light trains were ready for service in the spring of 1944, the heavy ones only at the end of 1944. For a time, in August of 1943, Armored Railcar No. 15, with six Panhard scout cars, was stationed in Greece as a substitute.

At the beginning of August 1943 the partisan activity behind the Army Group Center, which was fighting hard against the Russians who were attacking in a counter-stroke to the lost battle of Kursk, had taken on a threatening new dimension in the first use of row explosions of tracks, which crippled the transport traffic. In order to be able to deal with this danger, not only was the last armored train of the first series (No. 66) sent to the Army Group Center, but so were the first two of the second series (No. 67 to 72, as established by the OKH on April 27, 1943); No. 67 was ready for service by the end of August, No. 68 only in November.

After the Germans on the eastern front were pushed into a more and more defensive position, the armored trains took on another important task in addition to fighting partisans: corresponding to the other side's earlier experiences in 1941-42, they now proved their good fighting value on the defensive here too through their mobility and their variety of armament, especially as the Russian attacks were often aimed at breaking railroad connections to the rear. At the end of November 1942 — after the enclosing of Stalingrad — the armored trains in the Kharkov area (No. 7, 10 and 28) were all transferred to the Tschir bend (Oblivskaya —Cherniskov), where they gave support to the Stahel Battle Group, which was working to build up a defensive position. It was a time of costly defensive fighting until the withdrawal over the Donets took place in mid-January of 1943. Early in February of

1943, Armored Trains No. 7 and 28 continued the battle in Rostov; later they all met again in the Donets Basin to meet the constant Russian attempts to break the supply lines from Dniepropetrovsk. Only the names of Debalzevo (Armored Train No. 10), Krasnoarmeyskoye (No. 7 and 10) and Sinelnikovo (No. 7) can be named here. A time of relative calm followed the withdrawal fighting to the Dniepr after the lost battle of Kursk, which saw Armored Trains No. 11 (now a separate entity from No. 10), 28 and 62 active in the Kharkov area. The situation became particularly critical when the Russians broke through into the widespread area between Pripyet and Kiev, where scarcely any opposition to them could be offered, in November of 1943. Once again the armored trains and their mobile warfare were depended on.

Trains No. 7, 10 and 11 fought here along the Berditchev — Shitomir — Korosten line and gradually drew back through Sarny — Rovno — Shepetovka — Proskurov to Kovel — Brody — Tarnopol. — Armored Train No. 28 also had to withstand heavy fighting north of Krivoy Rog, as did No. 28 later on the western rim of the pocket at Cherkassy and near Uman. It is no wonder that, in view of this situation of the Army Group South, not only the rebuilt and strengthened No. 31 (October 1943, Shitomir — Berditchev — Kasatin area) and 30 (February 1944, to Nikolaiev - Odessa), but also the other second-series armored trains (the new No. 69 to 71, plus Armored Train No. 72 — see below), to this sector of the front. Meanwhile, though, serious organizational changes had also taken place. When the new General Inspection of the Panzer Troops, no longer subordinate to the Army General Staff and the Commander of the Replacement Army, had been created on April 1, 1943, the armored trains were given a mongrel status. They were, of course, regarded as part of the Panzer troops and subordinated to the Commander of Panzer Troops I in Insterburg, to whose realm Rembertow belonged, but the office of Commander of Railway Armored Trains (formerly Staff Officer of Railway Armored Trains under the General of the Fast Troops) remained — as a separate service-arm general, so to speak, and with a high degree of independence — in the Army General Staff. He retained command over the armored trains still back home in Germany (otherwise BdE!). In mutual agreement with the BdE, he could make changes in positions, send requests for equipment directly to the AHA and its In 6, and distribute available equipment on his own initiative. Training tasks as well as the preparation of requirements, memoranda and guidelines for the armored trains were handled by him on instructions from the Inspector General of the Panzer Troops. Only organizational realignments and the use of captured materials had to be routed to the Inspector General of the Panzer Troops and the Chief of Military Equipment and BdE. This indicates the importance that was now accorded to the armored trains. The Commander of the Railway Armored Trains was the former Staff Officer, Oberst von Olszewski, who held this office until it was abolished on March 31, 1945 (after that there was only an office of armored trains under the Inspector General of the Panzer Troops, a position filled by Major von Wedel).

Armored Trains No. 61 and 67 met on the Polozk-Vitebsk line in the spring of 1944.(SA)

In December of 1943 the number of armored trains had grown to almost thirty. With the Army Group North were Trains No. 51 and 63, with the Army Group Center No. 1, 2, 21, 27, 61, 66, 67 and 68, with the Army Group South No. 7, 10, 11, 28, 30, 31, 62, 69 and 70, in the Balkans No. 6, 23, 64 and 65, in France No. 22 and 25, while No. 3, 4, 24 and 26 were in back-line areas for repairs. At this point in time, two armored trains are missing from the list: No. 5 (abolished after being badly damaged on May 10, 1940) and No. 29 (blown up by its crew on January 13, 1942 on being cut off). This indicates the remarkable tenacity of this weapon type. The armored trains could certainly be damaged in a variety of ways, whether by mining the tracks, direct fire or bombardment, but in general only a part of the train was damaged, and as long as the tracks to the rear remained open, it could be withdrawn and repaired. Even the remains

of Armored Trains No. 10 and 27, which suffered badly in the surrounding of Kovel in March of 1944, were taken back to Rembertow after their liberation, though only No. 27 was rebuilt, No. 10 being abolished.

Only when an armored train was immobilized in the face of an advancing enemy through locomotive breakdown, derailment or breaking of the tracks did it have to be abandoned.

Such situations, of course, began to occur in growing numbers. On December 12, 1943 Armored Train No. 21 rolled into a Kasatin depot occupied by the enemy and had to be surrendered. Armored Train No. 69 was lost east of Tarnopol in March after it had been involved in a tank attack, shot up and derailed, and on April 4, 1944 — since all connections to the rear were broken — No. 70 had to be destroyed in Rasdelnaya. But the greatest loss was brought on by the collapse

of Army Group Center during the Russian summer offensive. From the end of June to the end of August 1944, Armored Trains No. 1, 28, 61 (with Railcar No. 17), 66 and 74 (after only a few days' service near Warsaw) were lost; at the same time, the Army Group North lost Armored Trains No. 51 and 67, and No. 63 was lost in the southern part of the eastern front. In September No. 71 was lost in Rumania, No. 32 in France and No. 304 (light scout train) in the Balkans.

These considerable losses could not be balanced at all by corresponding numbers of newly-made trains. In the nine months of 1944 before September 30, only four new armored trains went into service: No. 73 in Italy, 71, 74 (soon to be lost) and 75 (later Armored Training Train No. 5) on the eastern front; in addition, the four trains of light scout cars (No. 301 to 304) arrived in the Balkans, as did eight armored railcars (No.

16, 18, 19 and 20). This was all, although a large-scale program of new construction had been planned for 1944 (eight BP 44 armored trains, 16 heavy scout trains, 46 Panzerjäger cars (also for rearming older trains) and five armored railcars (this number was even exceeded by those made in Italy). The increasing lack of materials (by 1943 the Ukrainian steel mills, whose production had been available for the building of armored trains, had fallen into Russian hands) and weapons, plus the necessity of transferring needed personnel to other, more urgently needed services in view of the steadily worsening situation, led to increasingly long periods elapsing between the trains' authorization, establishment and readiness for service.

In the summer of 1944 these delays were surely lengthened by the fact that the armored train training and replacement unit had to be

The Commander of Armored Train No. 63, Oberleutnant Wesche, making an observation from the turret of his command car in the winter of 1943-44.(BA)

transferred from Rembertow to Milowitz (near Lissa, on the Elbe in northern Bohemia) at the end of July when the Russians approached Warsaw.

The armored trains were naturally rated at the second-highest level of urgency (along with the Panther and Tiger tanks!), and attempts were made to make sufficient supplies of steel available, but the program for 1944 had to be extended into the first quarter of 1945. In view of the high losses in the summer of 1944, essential doubts as to the value of armored trains surfaced, which caused considerable delays in building activity in the autumn of that year.

Thus only ten of the sixteen armored trains (heavy scout type) were established, the construction of two of them was halted again in January of 1945, and only two were ready for service before the beginning of 1945. Before this point too, only two of the BP 44 armored trains reached the troops, No. 76 in East Prussia and the new No. 75 in the Balkans (along with Armored Train No. 52, rebuilt from the track protection train "Blücher", which first saw service at Tilsit). The planned number of Panzerjäger cars (46) was not attained, which meant that the planned remarament of the older trains could not be carried out fully.

The Allied breakthrough from their beachhead in Normandy (as of July 25, 1944) and their landing on the Mediterranean coast of France (August 15, 1944) made the situation of the German armored trains stationed in southern France (No. 22, 24, 25 and 32) untenable. Despite the constant threat of air attack, the trains could be taken back to Germany with the exception of Armored Train No. 32, which had to be abandoned in St. Berain for lack of water. After appropriate rearming — particularly with Panzerjäger

An armored train of Standard Type BY 42 at firing drill on the shooting track of the Armored Train Replacement Unit at Rembertow.(SA)

cars — Armored Trains No. 22, 24 and 25 were transferred to Slovakia and southern Poland (October-November 1944). But the Wehrmacht was not spared further losses of armored trains in the last three months of 1944: Trains No. 3 and 21 in Courland and No, 6 plus Light Scout Trains No. 301 and 302 in the Balkans.

The year of 1944 also brought an organizational innovation. Until then, the armored trains had been turned over by the OKH to an army group or army, which had subordinated them to an appropriate unit in their area of command. Impractical subordinations and lack of understanding of the trains' unique qualities on the part of the commanders had often resulted in their service being detracted from, made useless or even predestined to failure. It also proved to be practical in defensive action to assemble several trains into a battle group, as had been done previously with Armored Train No. 10 but

then given up; this was advantageous not only in terms of heightened firepower, but also because of the possibility of mutual assistance, for example, the towing of an immobilized train. In order to manage all this as well as possible, it was decided to establish regimental staffs to command the armored trains within the individual army groups. One such position (Commander of the Armored Trains, Oberst Becker) had already been established in Army Group F (Balkans) in January of 1944. On the eastern front, where the army groups obviously could not all be set up with such staffs at once, a flexible solution was decided on. For this purpose, Armored Train No. 72 was divided that spring into two command trains, No. 72a and 72b, which were to serve as mobile command posts. Because of the high losses of armored trains, the practical installation of these staffs was much delayed. Armored Train Regimental Staff No. 2 (commanded by

Oberstleutnant von Türckheim at Altdorf, with Command Train No. 72a), with Army Group A (later Center) in Krakau, was set up only in November — after the French trains arrived in that area. Regimental Staff No. 3 (Oberstleutnant Dr. Günther, Command Train No. 72b) was established in October 1944 in East Prussia with Army Group Center (later North). The staff of Oberst Becker with Army Group F in the Balkans counted as No. 1.

After Regiment No. 3 had gone down to defeat at Gotenhafen in March of 1945, the staff with this number was reconstituted in the Army Group Center area (in Bohemia and Moravia) in the last days of the war, under the previous Commander of the Armored Train Replacement Unit, Major Naumann, though reliable information on it is lacking. The armored-train regimental staffs were intended to have their own command trains, consisting of command cars, anti-aircraft gun cars and Panzerjäger cars, but only Regimental Staff No. 1 received such a regulation train (No. I) in December of 1944; Staff No. 2 received only a makeshift train (No. II) in February of 1945, and another makeshift train (No. III) may have been available in April of 1945. In connection with these regimental staffs, four auxiliary railcars (directive of April 21, 1944) and two repair-shop trains (of which there is evidence of the actual use of only the first — No. 1, to Regimental Staff No. 1 in the Balkans on July 20, 1944) were authorized.

As 1945 began, the armored trains were divided at the fronts as follows: Army Group North (Courland): No. 26; Army Group Center: Command Train No. 72b, Trains 30, 52, 68, 76, Railcars No. 19, 21, 23; Army Group A: Command Train No. 72a, Trains No. 11, 22, 24, 25, 62, Railcars No. 16, 18, 20,

22; Army Group South: No. 64; Army Group F (Balkans): Trains No. 23, 75, 201, 202, 303, Railcars No. 15, 30 through 33, 35, 38; No. 65, coming from the Balkans, was being repaired in Milowitz. This list shows one concentration on the eastern front between the Baltic and the Carpathians, the other in the Balkans, but it also shows a difference: while the defensive assignments on the eastern front were suited to the regular armored trains with their strong artillery and the gun railcars (No. 18 to 23), the more lightly armed scout-car armored trains and light railcars (No. 15 and 30 to 38) predominated in the Balkans, where most of the fighting was against partisans or enemy troops not armed with many heavy weapons (for example, in Bulgaria).

When the Russian offensive began in mid-January of 1945, the few armored trains naturally could not hold the eastern front, which had been practically denuded of armored reserves for the benefit of the Ardennes offensive. South of Warsaw, only Command Train No. 72a and, at first, Armored Train No. 22, which was then in Slovakia, could avoid destruction, though No. 22 was later (February 11, 1945) given up near Sprottau; all the other trains stationed with Army Group A (later Center) were lost.

In East Prussia the situation was different. Here the Regimental Battle Group No. 2 (Oberstleutnant Dr. Günther) was originally in a quiet sector of the 4th Army (Command Train No. 72b, Armored Trains No. 30, 52, 68 and 76). Only when the Russian breakthrough into the 3rd Panzer Army and 2nd Ramy were obviously imminent (around January 20, 1945) were No. 72b and 30 ordered to the Soldau area; they were able to fight their way from there through Deutsch-Eylau, which was already surrounded, to

Photos of armored trains in action are very rare. The two on this page were taken during a display of Armored Train No. 76 for officers of the OKH at the Milowitz drill facility in October of 1944.(SA)

Marienburg (taking many refugees along). The operational half of Armored Train No. 68, which was in Königsberg for repairs, and Armored Train No. 52 also reached there. Only Armored Train No. 76 was cut off in Samland and lost there in April of 1945. The other four armored trains fought on in the Vistula lowlands, the Tucheler Heide and Far Pomerania, and were to be transferred to Lusatia early in March of 1945. But they were cut off by the Russian advance near Schlave and pushed back to Gotenhafen, where they were lost at the end of the month.

Early in February of 1945 the Armored Train Battle Group "Vistula" was set up to secure the Oder front east of Berlin; it was taken command of by Regimental Staff No. 2 (Oberstleutnant von Türckheim) — now using the makeshift Command Train No. II (originally at Fürstenwalde, later at Beenz, near Prenzlau).

The replacement unit at Milowitz could provide only Armored Training Train No. 5, the repaired No. 65, and the new No. 77; beyond that, track protection trains (No. 83 and "Max") had to be called in. The Inspector General of the Panzer Troops and the Reich Ministry for Armaments and War Production hastened to prepare the track protection train "Berlin", which was even equipped with Panther tanks. Later (in April of 1945) another track protection train, No. 350, which had been rebuilt in Berlin, was added, while "Max" was soon transferred to the Balkans. In addition, Railcars No. 22 and 37 joined the battle group, and later also No. 16 and 21. Armored Trains No. 72a (now functioning as a battle train again), 77 and Training Train No. 5 saw service in Pomerania and were lost there in late February and early March of 1945. All the vehicles of the battle group in action on the Oder were able to escape the

Russian offensive of mid-April 1945 except the track protection train "Berlin", which was destroyed by artillery fire. Armored Trains No. 65, 83 and 350 (plus No, 75, which was transferred from the Balkans to the area south of Berlin to protect the headquarters in Zossen and Wünsdorf), as well as Railcars No. 21 and 22 (No. 16 had to be abandoned south of Neu-Ruppin, and the fate of No. 37 is unknown) set out for Mecklenburg and surrendered to American units between Ludwigslust and Holthusen on May 2, 1945.

At the beginning of January 1945 it was decided to finish only the already begun armored trains, on account of material shortages. This decision did away with Armored Trains (heavy scout) No. 209 and

In the last year of the war, particular emphasis was placed on camouflaging the armored trains. Here camouflage is attached to the command half-train No. 72a in April of 1944.(SA)

210. With the enclosure of Breslau in February, the main production facility for armored trains, the Linke-Hofmann Works, was put out of production. The last known OKH order for the armored trains dates from April 5, 1945; it assigns personnel to Trains No. 81 and 82, stops work on No. 83 and 84 but calls for the quick completion of Panzerjäger Railcars No. 51 to 53, the auxiliary Command Train III and the track

protection trains No. 350, "Moritz" and "Werner", which were budgeted as auxiliary armored trains, as were "Berlin" and "Max" previously (and perhaps others?).

The last trains known to leave the replacement unit in Milowitz during the first few months of 1945 were Armored Trains No. 4, 78 and 79. They were all supposed to go to southwestern Hungary, but No. 4 was detoured to Croatia, as was the track protection train "Werner", which was built in Berlin. Of the armored trains stationed in southern Styria, Croatia and Slovenia in May of 1945, No. 4, 64 (with Railcar No. 19) and 78 were still able to reached Austrian territory, where their crews found safety with the western Allied occupying troops. For the other units (Armored Trains No. 23, 202, 203, 204 (heavy scout), 303 (light scout), track protection trains "Max", "München" and "Werner", Railcars No. 30, 31, 32, 34, 35, 38, Command Train No. 1 with the regimental staff, and Repair-Shop Train No. 1) there

was no more chance to make it through on the congested rail lines; they had to be turned over to Tito's troops, but some crew members fought their way through along the roads on the northern side of the Karawanken.

What happened to the Army Group Center in the last weeks of the war is still partially unexplained. In its area, Armored Trains No. 7, 27, 80, 81 and "Moritz", heavy scout trains No. 205 and 206 and Railcar No. 36 can be traced. But there were still other armored trains there. Among others, the numbers or names of two armored trains are unknown; one of them (under the command of Hauptmann Rudolf Dohms) surrendered to Czech units on May 5, 1945 and was used by the Czechs two or three days later to badly damage and beat back the other. In addition, shortly before the war ended, two other armored trains, hitherto unknown, are said to have operated in the Reichenberg area. On the other hand, it is unknown whether Armored Train No. 82 had been finished

before the war ended, and what happened to an Armored Train No. 99, the establishment of which is listed for April of 1945. After the capitulation, all the crews of these armored trains and the replacement unit — like all other German troops — tried to reach the Americans in the Pisek area. If they were not already caught by the advancing Russians, they experienced an unpleasant surprise there: they were all handed over to the Russians, and their fate was years of imprisonment.

Both pictures below:
Armored Train No. 62 in the battle to retake the railroad station at Chryplin (south of Stanislau) in March of 1944. (SA)

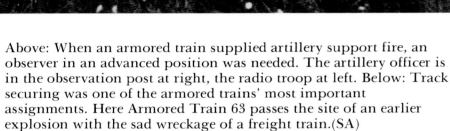

Above: When an armored train supplied artillery support fire, an observer in an advanced position was needed. The artillery officer is in the observation post at right, the radio troop at left. Below: Track securing was one of the armored trains' most important assignments. Here Armored Train 63 passes the site of an earlier explosion with the sad wreckage of a freight train.(SA)

Above: Russian women were also called in for repair work, under the protection of a standard-type armored train. Below: In November of 1943 Armored Train No. 68 was able to rescue and bring back a battalion enclosed south of the Berezina Pass near Shazilki.(SA)

Above: A heavy shell not only shattered the barrel of this 7.62-cm Field Cannon 295/l(r) on Armored Train No. 67, but also blew up the turret. Below: After Armored Train No. 1 had already been damaged in action, another bomb hit it in Vyasma on December 10, 1942. Afterward it was built up anew at the RAW facilities in Königsberg.(SA)

Above: On March 11, 1944 Armored Train No. 30 was rammed by an ammunition train at Lozinko (north of Nikolaiev). The pusher car was pushed up onto the tank-carrier car. Below: What remained of an armored train damaged in a fight with Russian tanks.(1 x SA, 1 x KR)

As of 1942, fighting the partisans who endangered supply lines was a main task of the armored trains. It was usually carried out by disembarked troops (pursuit commands) to the side of the railway line. Upper left: In the winter of 1942-43 an infantry troops with Russian sleds (aksyas) pushes into thick woods occupied by partisans northwest of Bryansk. Upper right: A grenade launcher provides support in an operation against partisans south of Welikiye Luki in the spring of 1942 (Armored Train No. 3). Lower left: The 38(t) tank of Armored Train No. 1 in action against a village occupied by partisans (spring 1944). Lower right: The village subsequently goes up in flames.(SA)

Above:
The pursuit command of Armored Train No. 2 has discovered a partisan camp in the central sector and destroyed it.(SA)

Upper right:
Three imprisoned Russians are transported to a prison camp on a pusher car in the Volkov area.(SA)

Right:
On June 19, 1943, three soldiers of Armored Train No. 63 fell in action against partisans east of the Novinka-Batezkaya line. They are being brought back to the train in tent cloths.

ARMAMENTS AND CREWS OF THE GERMAN ARMORED TRAINS

Zug Nr.	Offz.[1]	Uffz.	Mann	Pistolen	MPis	Gewehre	le.MG	s.MG	Gr.W.	Geschütze		Fahrräder
2	8	33	126	66	13	101	22	4	2	2:7,5 cm Geb.Kan.15 (ö/t)L/28	2:2 cm Flak	15
3	8	35	128	79	13	92	26	8	2	2:7,5 cm Vers.Gesch. L/41	2:2 cm Flak	15
4	7	34	136	69	12	108	18	4	2	2:4,7 cm Pak(h); 2:7,5 cm le.I.G.18	2:2 cm Flak	15
6[2]	7	34	112	76	13	77	20	2	2	4:7,62 cm FK 295/l(r)	2:2 cm Flak	19
7	8	33	132	70	13	103	26	4	2	2:7,5 cm Kan.02/26(p)	2:2 cm Flak	15
21	8	38	140	75	13	111	16	4	2	3:7,5 cm FK 02/26(p); 2:10 cm FH 14/19(p)	2:2 cm Flak	15
22	8	36	130	71	13	103	16	4	2	3:7,5 cm FK 02/26(p)	2:2 cm Flak	15
23, 24	8	33	125	67	13	99	16	4		2:7,5 cm Gb.Kan.15(ö/t)L/28	2:2 cm Flak	15
25[3]	6	30	98	77	15	60	16	1	2	2:7,5 cm Gb.Kan.15 (ö/t)L/28	2:2 cm Flak	15
26-28	6	28	98	65	14	76	12+3			3 Pz.Somua S35 mit 1:4,7 cm KwK u. 1MG	2:2 cm Flak	15
29-31	6	27	95	52	13	76	12+2			2 Pz.Somua S35 mit 1:4,7 cm KwK u. 1MG	2:2 cm Flak	15
27[4]	7	35	120	69	13	93	18+2		2	4:7,62 cm FK 295/l(r); 2 Pz.Somua S35	2:2 cm Flak	15
10a	2	13	62	46	4	31	19			2:7,5 cm FK02/26(p); 2:10 cm FH 14/19(p)	1:2 cm Flak	
10b	2	13	62	46	4	31	19			4:7,5 cm FK 02/26(p)	1:2 cm Flak	
10cpl. (+ Fhr/Troß)	9	49	158	113	8	102	38			wie oben	wie oben	24
51[4]	6	27	84	60	9	57	10+4		2	4 Pz.Türme mit 4,5 cm KwK(r) u. 1MG	1:4x2 cm Flak	14

All armored trains also had: 3 antitank guns, 1 flamethrower; as reconnaissance vehicles: 1 armored railcar, 1 rail motorcycle; as supply vehicles: 1 1.5-ton truck, 1 car, 1 billet train.

Information from K.St.N./K.A.N. of January-February 1942, except [2]August 42, [3]March 44, [4]May 1942; [1]Officers included 1 paymaster; light machine guns: number after + sign = built-in.

Notes: Armored Trains No. 1 to 7 (ex-track protection) 1939: all 6-10 heavy 08 MG, 4 MG 34 (AA twins); No. 1, 2, 5: no other heavy armament, 130 men.

No. 3, 4, 6, 7: 2 7.5-cm guns, some grenade launchers, 150-160 men.

Armored Trains No. 26 to 28 (29 to 31) June 1944: in addition to Somua tanks: 6 rifles, 4(3) machine pistols, 12 (9) pistols; 1 officer, 5(4) NCO, 16(13) men. Most of these earlier armored trains were rearmed and upgraded many times. In 1943-44 those still in service, with the exception of No. 22 and 51, were made equal to the K.St.N./K.A.N. standard type BP 42 or BP 44.

	Offz.	Uffz.	Mann	Pistolen	MPis	Gewehre	le.MG	s.MG	weitere Waffen und Fahrzeuge
EINHEITSPANZERZUG BP 42 (K.St.N./K.A.N. 1.2.43):									
Führer-Gruppe (+San., Nachr.Tr. u. Troß)	3[1]	9	18	11	4	19	2+2		2 Panhard 38(f) armored scout cars with 1 25mm KwK and 1 MG, 1 car, a 1.5-ton truck, 3 bicycles.
1. Zug (zugl. Stoßtrupp)	1	9	41	32	5	19	8	1	See below.
s.MG-Trupp		2	7	6	1	3		1	
Gr.W.-Gruppe		2	8	6	1	4			2 8-cm grenade launchers, 3 antitank guns, 6 bicycles,
le.MG-Gruppe		3	17	16	1	4	6		6 bicycles,
Pi-Gruppe		2	9	3	1	8	2		1 flamethrower, 4 bicycles.
2. Zug	1	12	33	28	3	18	6+4		see below.
Art.-Gruppe		6	17	18	1	12	4		2 7.62-cm FK 295/l(r), 2 10-cm FH 14/19(p); [2]
Flak-Gruppe		2	12	8		6	2		2 quadruple 2-cm Flak
Panzer-Gruppe		4	4	8	2		+4		2 38(t) tanks with 1 37mm KwK and 2 MG.
Techn.Bes. (Reichsbahn)	1	5	3	6	3	3			
BP 42 in total	6[1]	35	95	77	15	59	16-6	1	see above

[1] Officers include [1]paymaster; [2]or 4 7.62-cm or 10-cm guns, light machine guns: number after + sign: built-in.

	Offz.	Uffz.	Mann	Pistolen	MPis	Gewehre	le.MG	s.MG	weitere Waffen und Fahrzeuge
UNIFORM ARMORED TRAIN BP 44 (K.St.N./K.A.N.) 8/1/44):									
Führer-Gruppe (+San. u. Nachr.)	2	4	12	3	2	13			
Pz.Grenadier-Zug:	1	6	41	12	7	29	4	2	See below.
2 Pz.Gren.-Gruppen		2	22	6	2	16	2	2	12 bicycles.
Gr.W.-Gruppe		2	8	4	2	4			28mm Grenade Launcher 34.
Pz.Pi.-Gruppe		1	9	2	1	7	2		1 flamethrower.
Pz.- u. Aufklärungs-Gruppe		5	7	9	3		+5		See below.
Pz.-Gruppe		4	4	6	2		+4		2 38(t) tanks with 37mm KwK and 2 MG.
Aufkl.Gruppe		1	3	3	1		+1		1 Panhard 38(f) armored scout car with 1 25mm KwK & 1 MG.
Pz.Zug-Batterie	1	6	17	10	2	12	4		4 10.5-cm light FH 18/40.
Pz.Flak-Halbzug		2	12	8		6	2		2 quadruple 20mm Flak.
s.Pz.Jäger-Halbzug		2	4	4	2				2 tank turrets with 75mm KwK 40 L/48.
Techn.Bes. (Reichsbahn)	1	5	3	3		6			
Troß	1[1]	5	6	1	2	9	2		1 car, 1 2-ton truck.
BP 44 in total	6[1]	35	102	50	18	75	12+5	2	see above
PANZERZUG(s.Sp.) (K.St.N./K.A.N. 1.8.44)									
1 Wg.: Führer (San.. Nachr.)	2	8	9	10	3	6	+2		1 Panhard 38(f) armored scout car with 1 25mm KwK & 1 MG.
1. Zug (Inf.)	1	6	41	14	7	27	6+4	1	See below.
1 Wag.: Führer	1	1	2	1	2	1	+1		
2 Wag.: MG- u. Gr.W.Gruppe		4	28	10	4	18	4+2	1	2 8-cm 34 Grenade Launchers.
1 Wag.: Pi-Gruppe		1	11	3	1	8	2+1		1 41 Flamethrower.
2. Zug (Art.)	1	12	38	34	9	8	+9		See below.
1 Wg.: Führer	1	2	4	3	2	2	+1		
2 Wg.: Art.-Gruppe		2	8	6	2	2	+2		2 7.5-cm KwK L/24.
2 Wg.: Gr.W.-Gruppe [2]		2	8	6	2	2			2 8-cm 34 or 10-cm 42 grenade launchers.
2 Wg.: Flak-Gruppe[3]		2	14	13	1	2	+2		2 quadruple 20mm Flak.
2 Wg.: Pz.-Gruppe [4]		4	4	6	2		+4		2 38(t) tanks with 1 37mm KwK & 2 MG.
Troß	1[1]	6	7	2	2	10	2		1 car, a 2-ton truck, 2 bicycles.
Armored train (heavy scout) in total	5[1]	32	95	60	21	51	8+15	1	see above

Later addition: Technical crew 2 NCO, 3 men, 2 pistols, 3 rifles for steam locomotive.
[1] includes 1 paymaster, [2] later omitted, [3] on low-side cars, [4] on tank-carrier car, light MG: Number after + sign: built-in.

	Offz.	Uffz.	Mann	Pistolen	MPis	Gewehre	le.MG	s.MG	weitere Waffen und Fahrzeuge
PANZERZUG (le.Sp.) (K.St.N./K.A.N. 1.10.43):									
1 Wg.: Führer (+San. u.Nachr.)	1	2	2	4	2	1	4		
1 Wg.: Führer (2.Zughälfte)	1	1	4	5	1	1	4		
6 Wg.: Infanterie		6	30	30	6	6	24		
2 Wg.: Pioniere		2	10	10	2	2	8		
Troß		5	7	3		9			1 PKW, 1 LKW(1,5to), 1 Fahrrad
Panzerzug (le.Sp.) insgesamt	2	16	53	52	11	19	40		siehe Aufschlüsselung oben
PANZER-TRIEBWAGEN									
Panzer-Triebwagen Nr. 15	1	8	17	12	3	11	6		1 bicycle.
Panzer-Triebwagen Nr. 30−38(Ansaldo ALn-56)		7	23	13	9	8	2+6		2 tank turrets with 47mm KwK & 1 MG, 1 2-cm Flak, 1 grenade launcher.
Panzer-Geschütz-Triebwagen Nr. 16−23	1	8	12	10	3	8	2		2 7.62-cm FK 295/1(r) or 2 10-cm FH 14/19(p).
Panzerjäger-Triebwagen Nr. 51−53	1	8	12	10	3	8	2		2 tank turrets with 75mm KwK L/48, 1 bicycle.

THE GERMAN ARMORED TRAINS OF WORLD WAR II IN CHRONOLOGICAL ORDER

Pz.Zug Nr.	Aufstellg.	verw.ber.	Einsatzräume (6.41-5.45)	Umbau[1]	Verbleib		
1	26. 8.39	16. 9.39	M	12.42- 8.43	a/g	27. 6.44	Bobruisk
2	8. 9.39	13. 9.39	M	7.44-	z	18. 7.44	Neubau unfertig
3	5. 7.39	25. 8.38	M; 9.44:N	8.43- 7.44	a/g	10.10.44	Vainoden
4	11. 8.39	8.39	S; 7.42:M; 1.45:B	12.43- 1.45	k	10. 5.45	Kärnten
5	8.39	9.39			b/z	10. 5.40	Roermond
6	10. 7.39	8.39	N; 9.42:B	5.- 9.42	v	1.10.44	o Betschkerek
7	1. 8.39	8.39	S; 4.45:P	3.44- 4.45	l	9. 5.45	Böhmisch-Trübau
23	1. 3.40	4.40	B	10.42- 8.43	l	9. 5.45	Unterdrauburg
24	1. 3.40	4.40	B; 2.44:I; 7.44:F; 10.44:A	3.43- 1.44	a/g	16. 1.45	o Konskie
25 (ex 9)	1. 3.40	4.40	1.42:M; 11.42:F; 11.44:A	9. -11.44	v	13. 1.45	sw Kielce
21	10. 6.40	22. 7.40	F; 10.42:M; 9.44:N		e	30.10.44	Moscheiken
22	10. 7.40	8.40	F; 10.44:A/M		v	11. 2.45	Sprottau
26	1. 6.41	22. 6.41	N/K	3.43- 2.44	k	9. 5.45	Libau
27	1. 6.41	22. 6.41	M; 4.45:P	4.44- 4.45	k	9. 5.45	Böhmen-Mähren
28	1. 6.41	22. 6.41	M; 3.42:S; 5.44:M	12.43- 3.44	a/g	29. 6.44	bei Krupki
29	1. 6.41	22. 6.41	M		a/g	10. 1.42	w Kaluga
30	1. 6.41	22. 6.41	N; 2.44:S; 8.44:M; 10.44:O	11.42- 2.44	e	21. 3.45	bei Groß-Katz
31	1. 6.41	22. 6.41	S	11.42-10.43	e	28.12.43	Kasatin
10(a)	1.12.41	2. 2.42	S		b/z	21. 3.44	Kowel
51[2] (ex Stettin)	16. 6.42		N		b/g	13. 8.44	Somerpalu
61	1. 9.42	23.12.42	M		a/g	27. 6.44	Bobruisk
62	1. 9.42	11. 2.43	S; 8.44:A		a/g	16. 1.45	o Konskie
63	1.10.42	1. 5.43	N; 4.44:S		v	17. 7.44	w Krasne
64	1.10.42	18. 6.43	B; 11.44:U		l	9. 5.45	bei Leoben
65	1.11.42	11. 7.43	B; 2.45:W		k	2. 5.45	Holthusen
66	1.11.42	23. 7.43	M		a/g	30. 7.44	o Siedlce
67	15. 5.43	22. 9.43	M; 1.44:N		b/g	27. 7.44	s Mitau
68	1. 8.43	3.11.43	M; 10.44:O		g	31. 3.45	Oxhöft
11(ex 10b)	1. 8.43	1. 8.43	S/A	3.- 7.44	v	13. 1.45	sw Kielce
69	20. 8.43	8.11.43	S		v	22. 3.44	o Tarnopol
70	16. 9.43	8.12.43	S		a/g	4. 4.44	Rasdelnaja
71	16. 9.43	12. 1.44	S; 5.44:R		a/g	31. 8.44	Slanic
301(le.Sp.)	16. 9.43	29. 2.44	B		a/g	30.11.44	Kraljevo
302(le.Sp.)	16. 9.43	19. 3.44	B		v	12.11.44	Kosovo Polje
303(le.Sp.)	16. 9.43	14. 6.44	B		k	9. 5.45	Cilli
304(le.Sp.)	16. 9.43	22. 4.44	B		a/g	30. 8.44	Lavara
72a(Kdo.)	23.11.43	20. 2.44	11.44:A; 2.45:W		a/g	10. 3.45	Kolberg
72b(Kdo.)	23.11.43	20. 2.44	10.44:O		g	31. 3.45	Oxhöft
73	19.11.43	17. 6.44	I		l	2. 5.45	Udine
201(s.Sp.)	5. 1.44	11.11.44	B		a/g	15. 4.45	Cacinci
202(s.Sp.)	10. 1.44	11.11.44	B		k	9. 5.45	Kronau
203(s.Sp.)	21. 2.44	18. 1.45	B		k	9. 5.45	Schönstein
204(s.Sp.)	23. 3.44	6. 2.45	B		k	9. 5.45	bei Cilli
32	17. 4.44	12. 7.44	F		e	8. 9.44	St. Berain
74	20. 3.44	15. 7.44	M		v	28. 7.44	vor Otwock
Lehr 5 (ex 75)	15. 4.44	15. 7.44	M; 10.44:O; 2.45:W		a/g	5. 3.45	Belgard
76	4. 4.44	18.11.44	O		b/g	15. 4.45	Seerappen
77	1. 5.44	19. 1.45	W		v	26. 2.45	o Bublitz
205(s.Sp.)	4. 4.44	4.45	P		l	9. 5.45	Lissa
206(s.Sp.)	17. 4.44	4.45	P		k	9. 5.45	Milowitz

Pz.Zug Nr.	Aufstellg.	verw.ber.	Einsatzräume	Verbleib		
52[2] (ex Blücher)	1. 6.44	10.10.44	O	e	21. 3.45	bei Groß-Katz
78	25. 5.44	6. 2.45	U	l	9. 5.45	bei Judenburg
79	10. 7.44	6. 2.45	U	a/g	27. 3.45	w Celldömölk
80	7. 8.44	4.45	P	k	9. 5.45	Böhmen-Mähren
81	16. 9.44	4.45	P	k	9. 5.45	Böhmen-Mähren
75	23.10.44	31.12.44	B; 2.45:W	k	2. 5.45	Holthusen

Established before the war ended, but service and fate unknown (not finished?): Armored Trains No. 82 and 99, heavy Scout Trains No. 207 amd 208. Construction of Armored Trains Mo. 83 and 84 and light Scout Trains 209 and 210 was cancelled before the war ended.

Command Trains No. I (12/44 B, k 5/9/45 near Cilli); No. II (2/45 W, w 5/12/45 w Grevesmühlen); No. III (4/45 P?).

In service with S 2-3/44: Training Train R of Armored Train Replacement Unit (Type BP 42), b 3/9/44 at Tarnopol, no further data.

Track protection trains taken over 2-2/45: "Berlin" (2/45 W, v 4/16/45 Seelow); "Max" (2/45 B, k 5/9/45 near Cilli); "Moritz" (3/45 P. k 5/9/45 Bohemia-Moravia); "Werner" (2/45 B, k 5.9.45 near Cilli); No. 83 (2/45 W, k 5/2/45 Holthusen); No. 350 (4/45 W, k 5/2/45 Holthusen).

Footnotes: [1] Rebuilt according to K.St.N./K.A.N. standards for BP 42 or BP 44.
[2] Former track protection train.

Abbreviations:
Areas:
A = Army Group A (Poland 44-45), B = Balkans, F = France, I = Italy, K = Courland (44-45), M = Army Group Center, N = Army Group North, O = East Prussia (44-45), P = Protectorate of Bohemia and Moravia (45), R = Rumania, S = Army Group South (including all others in southern section of eastern front: A, B, Don, North and South Ukraine), U = Hungary, W = Army Group Vistula (45).

Fate:
a = cut off, b = damaged, e = captured by enemy, g = blown up by crew, k = surrendered, l = abandoned, v = destroyed by enemy action, z = taken out of service.

Oberst Egon von Olszewski, Staff Officer of the Armored Trains under the General of the *Schnelle Truppen*, later Commander of the Armored Trains in the OKH.(SA)

THE GERMAN RAILCARS OF WORLD WAR II

Car No.	Established	Completed	Subordinate to Train No.	Area	Fate
15	8.39	9.39	7, 25, 6 304, 65	40:F; 12.41:M; 3.43:B	k 9. 5.45 Graz
16	27. 1.44	44	11, 83, 350	A/M; 2.45:W	e 2. 5.45 bei Neustadt/Dosse
17	10. 4.43	7.12.43	61	M	a/g 27. 6.44 Bobruisk
18	20.11.43	14. 7.44	(63), 11	S/A	e 16. 1.45 Kielce
19	20.11.43	30. 8.44	30, 64	M; 10.44:O; 3.45:U	l 9. 5.45 bei Leoben
20	20.11.43	18. 9.44	62	A	e 20. 4.45 Nürnberg
21	27. 1.44	10.10.44	52, 83	O; 3.45:W	k 2. 5.45 Holthusen
22	27. 1.44	26.10.44	22, 65	A/M; 2.45:W	k 2. 5.45 Holthusen
23	27. 1.44	18.11.44	76	O	g 15. 4.45 Seerappen
30	12. 5.44	17. 6.44	303	B	k 9. 5.45 Cilli
31	12. 5.44	17. 6.44	303	B	k 9. 5.45 Cilli
32	12. 5.44	12. 7.44	(302), 64, 65, 4?	B.	k 9. 5.45 Slowenien
33	12. 5.44	12. 7.44	(302), 64, 65	B	e 20. 4.45 Nürnberg
34	21. 8.44	11.11.44	204	B	l 9. 5.45 bei Cilli
35	21. 8.44	11.11.44	23	B	k 9. 5.45 Unterdrauburg
36	21. 8.44	4.45		P	k 6. 5.45 Böhmen-Mähren
37	21. 8.44	1. 2.45		W	unbekannt
38	21. 8.44	11.11.44	?	B	k 9. 5.45 Cilli
51–53	4.45				Herstellerwerk Steyr

Abbreviations as in the previous table.

On the day of surrender, May 9, 1945, the crews leave Armored Train (light scout) No. 303 and its Armored Railcars No. 30 and 31 at Cilli (Celje).

Inspection of armored trains south of Polozk, late April 1944. Second from right: Oberleutnant (later Hauptmann) Hoppe, Commander of Armored Train No. 67; third from right: Oberstleutnant von Türckheim, later Commander of Armored Trains in Army Group A (Armored Train Regimental Staff No. 2); fifth from right: (in profile, with peaked cap and pistol holster) Hauptmann Fischer, Commander of Armored Train No. 26; far left: Leutnant Sitzius, Commander of Command Train No. 72a. In the background is Armored Train No. 26.(SA)

1.

Armored Trains 1-7
Armored Trains 23-25

Gun cars and car parks very similar, but consisted of captured Czech cars (partly from pre-1918 Austria)

2.

Armored Trains 10(11), 21, 22

Train 21: plus 1-turret gun car
Train 22: instead of a 2-turret,
only a 1-turret gun car

3.

Armored Trains 26-31   No infantry car in No. 30 & 31

No tank carrier car in No. 29-31

4.

Armored Trains 1-31   Rebuilt to K.St.N. 1169x, some with Panzerjäger cars instead of pushers

5.

Type BP 42/44   BP 42 without Panzerjäger cars

6.

Armored Trains (heavy Scout) 201-210

7.

Armored Trains (light scout) 301-304

Composition of German Armored Trains from 1941 to 1945